FLORAL
HOUSE

FLORAL HOUSE

simple designs and decorations for the home

Julia Bird

photographs by **Pia Tryde**

text by **Jane Newdick**

CHRONICLE BOOKS

SAN FRANCISCO

For dearest Madeleine
       . . . mudilly Madilly

First published in the United States
in 2001 by Chronicle Books LLC

Frances Lincoln Limited
4 Torriano Mews
Torriano Avenue
London NW5 2RZ

Library of Congress Cataloging-in-
Publication Data available.

ISBN 0-8118-3093-4

Printed in Singapore

Cover design by Adam George

Distributed in Canada by
Raincoast Books
9050 Shaughnessy Street
Vancouver, British Columbia V6P 6E5

10 9 8 7 6 5 4 3 2 1

Chronicle Books LLC
85 Second Street
San Francisco, CA 94105

www.chroniclebooks.com

contents

Swatches of paints

and fabrics provide

a starting point for

a new decorative

scheme.

introduction

Simple floral ideas, used with economy and restraint, turn a house into a home.

They bring interiors to life, adding warmth and vitality, and create a look that is

dynamic and different, yet extremely easy to live with.

RIGHT

Flowers do not have to be lavish or exotic. A couple of elegant stems in a clear vase bring an otherwise plain room to life, proving that simplicity is the key to success.

I have always loved flowers and floral patterns – I can still vividly recall pretty flowery frocks I wore as a young child. My school years passed filling the margins of my exercise books with fantastic floral images; a little later, I began searching through charity and junk shops for vintage flowery curtains to cut down into my trademark dirndl skirt and, once I owned my own flat, to hunt around for oddly shaped dresses that could be transformed into pillowcases or cushions, and for oddments of floral china and other eclectic bric-à-brac. Even now, my travels abroad involve tracking down local fabrics, ceramics and hardware, and the best part of coming home is unpacking these treasures and then arranging them around the house.

This book is about providing the key to creating a new floral look, in which just a few floral fabrics or accessories are displayed to great effect against a neutral background, in which natural materials – wood, glass and ceramics – play a textural role. The more neutral in tone the overall room, the easier it is to introduce floral pattern. Imagine a stark white interior and then, in your mind's eye, throw a brightly colored floral tablecloth over the table: the room is instantly enlivened and imbued with personality. This look is about adding highlights of color and pattern, and creating interesting contrasts of style, for an understated, balanced, but extremely easy to live with, look.

The key is to start with a floral fabric that you love, and then use it to make a single statement. Avoid clutter and arrange things in a simple, elegant way. Try, for instance, combining a lean contemporary sofa with antique chairs, add vintage floral cushions and then highlight the colors in the fabric with a few fresh flowers or reverse this process in a country setting, using a modern floral fabric and an occasional item of sleek, modern, metal furniture.

An otherwise plain room can be cheered up with bold, splashy floral fabrics, or a single large glass bowl of fresh flowers could make the only soft accent in an otherwise hard-edged modern interior. A traditional tiny sprigged print would instantly soften the feel of a contemporary sofa, while classic dining chairs would look fresh and new covered in a modern, abstract floral.

As flowers provide us with some of the most subtle and beautiful images in nature, they offer the essential finishing touch to any room. Their form and colors change through the seasons, from the unfurling fresh pale green leaves of spring, and bright and brilliant flowers of summer through to the misty heads of dying flowers in autumn. This book takes its inspiration, in part, from these seasonal changes and also shows how to contrast form and texture, as well as color, in ways that surprise and delight. Remember that a single flower or two will have more impact (and is more economical) than a lavish bunch, but use containers imaginatively and keep the displays informal and natural looking: old zinc florists' buckets and contemporary glass vases provide just the right kind of look.

I hope this book inspires you to look around you with a fresh eye, so that you enjoy, as much as I have, finding new ways to display flowers and floral patterns that both echo your personality and bring new life into your surroundings.

LEFT

A vivid floral print
on a strong blue
background makes
a plump cushion that
brings a plain and
simple wooden kitchen
chair to life. The neat
striped cotton seat
contrasts totally but
is connected by the
deep coral pink color
in both fabrics.

fresh and light

The clear colors of spring, leaf greens and sunny yellows,

lift the pale neutrals of warm creams and blonde wood.

Yellow can be a difficult color to use in interiors but the

right amount in the right shade brings vitality to a room –

a flash of sunlight caught through vivid new leaves.

Neutral colors are usually assumed to be a safe and easy decorating option. Off-whites, pale creams, blondes and shades of taupe are always pleasing to the eye but used indiscriminately they can, if not carefully controlled, become bland and unexciting. The cool cream interior has become almost a modern interior cliché – it always looks sophisticated but often cries out for a spark of some other color to give the whole scheme some character. The clever and contemporary way to use neutrals is to add hints of sharper light colors, such as dashes of citrus yellows and limes. To achieve the right shade, think of the fresh green of an unfurling beech leaf or the color of a stem of spring grass caught in the sunlight.

Rich golden egg-yolk yellows or warm buttery shades look magnificent with pale neutrals as long as you keep to a neutral range that has no pink or blue in its make-up. Those cooler creams that are nearer to stone than to pinky mushroom beige are easier to combine with these particular sharp light greens and yellows. The yellow citrus shades are probably best added in small amounts as definition. They will then add a freshness and feel of the outdoors like no other color can. Take your cue from the yellow of spring tulips or from late summer sunflowers, from the saturated gold of buttercups and the subtler hues of black-eyed Susans and daylilies. We are used to living with the greens of nature in larger amounts so even the most vivid grassy green can be soothing in an interior, reminding us as it does of fields, trees and a wider landscape. Opt for greens that have plenty of yellow in their make-up and avoid those that veer towards blue and turquoise, especially if you are combining them with yellow in a predominantly neutral scheme.

The more buttery yellows will warm up a classically cool interior. A bold floral with large areas of pure clean color off-setting splashy blooms has a truly modern edge and brings a neutral interior to life. Using different colors of the same design to cover two chairs works well when the rest of the room is clean and simple. While one could have a warm ochre yellow background to its large flower pattern, the second might have a cooler beige. Although they might have different colors for the flower pattern, the same green used for the leaves would connect the two fabrics.

Fabrics with bold prints are generally best treated in a very simple way. Old-fashioned armchairs can be transformed by simple floral loose covers if the fabric is chosen with care. Huge painterly roses can be the focus of attention provided the construction of the cover itself does not detract from the impact of the print. Chair covers, for example, should be constructed in a neat but slightly loose style that allows the pattern to be shown to advantage. The minimal route is generally the best one to take with patterned soft furnishings because they rarely require any extra fussy detailing or trimming. From a purely practical point of view cushions, curtains, throws and bed covers should be finished as plainly as possible which makes them easy to live with and simple to launder or have cleaned. Loose covers look more contemporary without piping, especially if the fabric is a traditional floral pattern, although some chairs with finer detailing may need traditional piping to help define the shape. Much will depend on the weight and texture of the fabric used. Finishing the hem of the cover to leave the legs showing adds to the contemporary feel. The space left under the cover prevents them from looking too solid or heavy.

RIGHT

Outsize roses bloom
across a glorious fabric
used in two different
colors on two similar
but not identical
armchairs. The covers
are simple, loose and
thoroughly modern.

RIGHT

A decisively modern sitting room in a handsome Edwardian house combines traditional style with modern simplicity. A splash of bright color is introduced with the pair of Louis XV chairs covered in a bright lemon and lime cotton fabric, while a simple arrangement of delicate yellow spray orchids reiterates the restrained elegance of the scheme.

Strong colors, such as bright egg yolk yellow, need to be kept under careful control. One of my favourite prints, a wonderful large-scale vintage Sanderson chintz from the 1950s, employs it in a design based on branches of mimosa in full bloom accented with sprays of the fern-like leaves. At the time that this design was in production a fabric such as this was more likely to have been used as curtains than just as an accent of color and pattern in a simpler scheme. Now our taste is for using less pattern but increasing its impact by showcasing it against the simplicity of a piece of modern furniture.

Different colors of the same fabric can be employed in one scheme, if you handle them with care. Used to cover large cushions so that the bold design is really seen to its best advantage, these fabrics could become the focal point of an otherwise neutral living room, in which a sofa or chair might be upholstered in plain beige fabric. Take away the cushions and the whole scheme falls flat, but with the addition of touches of boldly patterned floral fabric the room immediately becomes animated and lively. To give the room unity, the colors in the cushions could pick up those used in a large flower painting, for example, positioned on a facing wall.

Old color swatches or short lengths of vintage fabric can still be found in antique shops and markets and are perfect for copying this simple but effective idea. A range of colors of one pattern may not appear to work together but because the designer's color palette is likely to have been tonally similar for every design, there is usually a strong connecting link between even quite different versions.

The golden blooms
of butterfly orchid
are an intensely
saturated color.

THIS PAGE

Brilliantly patterned
cushions catch the
eye on a plain sofa.

FAR LEFT

Kitchen cupboards
have been painted in
a glorious sunny yellow
inspired by the color
of black-eyed Susans
and sunflowers. Though
it might seem a bold
choice of color for
a busy room, yellow
rarely overpowers the
senses, unlike more
vibrant shades of red
and orange.

LEFT

A simple gray stone
bowl throws the golden-
yellow daisies into
sharp relief.

Yellow creates a very special mood in a room but certain shades are difficult to use in large quantities, especially those that have an acid edge and are moving towards green in the color spectrum. Easier to live with and use with other colors are the warmer, buttery yellows that have a hint of orange in their make-up: think of bananas and egg yolks, honey-colored wood and sandy beaches. In nature this warm yellow shade is quite rare; many more flowers are a clearer golden yellow or a very bright and luminous, almost lemony shade. This softer yellow, however, is not only easy on the eye but also quite assertive, generating its own warmth. Use it in a cold or severe-looking space to bring it to life but surround it with plenty of space and light. It combines well with metals or bleached wood and looks best when white or very pale shades of cream are used with it to dilute the overall effect.

Some rooms, even when the light streams in, can sometimes have quite a cold and gray feel, particularly during the winter months. Yellow is an excellent choice to counteract this. In a modern bedroom, for example, with an elegant stripped wood floor, you could make a feature of a centrally placed simple but elegant bed, covering its spare lines with plain butter-yellow sheets and using blankets to add a counter-balancing softness and sensuousness. A simple panel blind, perhaps edged with yellow, could hang at the windows. Offset any tendency to starkness by using attractively rounded tables and chairs, in pale bleached wood, but take care not to overfurnish the room and lose its sleek simplicity. A contemporary glass vase, with a few really sumptuous, large-petalled flowers in golds and greens, would give the room a more feminine feel.

Muted floral
bedlinen in soft
yellow brings an
elegantly simple
bedroom to life.

1 A magnetic stainless steel bulletin board is the perfect way to display favourite floral images from art postcards to scraps of fabric in an ever-changing reference library of ideas **2** A green enameled vase used to store bathroom brushes and bottles of shampoo or washing-up paraphernalia brings color to a plain room **3** Twiggy stems of spring blossom with definite Japanese overtones are just the right match for this modern ceramic vase **4** A purely practical all-white tiled bathroom benefits from the frivolity of an over-sized crêpe paper flower twisted over the mirror frame **5** Delicately painted floral tea glasses would look pretty filled with a pale herb tisane **6** Flower-shaped glass light-holders burn with a strong golden glow when lit

bright ideas

There is no better way of enlivening a room than adding

accents of warm yellow. It has the knack of lifting the spirits

like no other color, bringing verve and vitality to an interior

in the way that sunshine does.

5

4

6

Mixing different floral fabrics in the past was usually a fairly safe affair. Colors were carefully put together and intended to match and enhance each other, and the floral designs usually came from the same historic period or plant references. The variables tended to be only in the pattern scale, with large flowery images combined with some medium-sized ones and perhaps a tiny simple all-over floral motif. This look was quite easy to achieve but ran the risk that it could easily become bland and predictable, reminiscent of a featureless hotel bedroom.

These days we mix and match our clothes more experimentally and it is time to carry this sense of adventure into interior fabric choices and combinations, too. The variables of texture, scale, color, type of print or weave, style of design and image can all be played around with, allowing us to create a totally personal look.

The hardest decision to make is where to start. Begin with a fabric you love so that you do not get tired of it too soon. Floral designs have all kinds of connotations and resonances: some of us will instinctively go for traditionally painted blowsy roses and country garden flowers while others want their florals harder edged and more sophisticated, abstract and contemporary.

When it comes to color mixing, look out for examples where you think color combinations have worked, in fashion, nature, paintings and, of course, fresh flowers. Keep pictures of things that you like and that inspire you on a bulletin board or in a scrap book as a reference for the times when you want to experiment and try your ideas out for real.

LEFT

Here a lime-green floral cardigan folded over a striking black and white wool throw on a chair-back demonstrates how different kinds of floral pattern and texture can contrast successfully, if surprisingly.

In an uncompromisingly modern interior, parrot-green chrysanthemum heads float with Zen-like simplicity in a clear glass bowl. The sharp green flowers and simple graphic china provide a suitable color accent. Each of the plain dinner plates has a different botanical motif as decoration – the one concession to femininity in this smartly severe interior.

fresh and light

Brightly colored flowers,

simply arranged, create

a human touch

in this sleek and

streamlined stainless

steel and white kitchen.

Green floral majolica plates, Chinese glazed earthenware (part of a well-loved collection of plates bought years ago), together with a few brightly colored tulips, add personality to the practical kitchen shelves.

China decorated with floral images has, like fabric, moved a long way from the meticulous hand-painted bouquets of the eighteenth century or the busy, chintzy patterns of the 1930s and '40s. Now you can have a sculptural, minimalist piece that is as much about line and form as it is about decoration although the inspiration has probably still come from nature. All styles of floral china have their place even in the simplest contemporary interior. As ever, it is about choosing one or two exceptional pieces that you love, and displaying them in a complementary way. Large collections of matching china look out of place these days and who wants to dust them all anyway?

But in the same way that fabric brings images of flowers into the home, decorated china allows you to bring color and floral detail into neutral surroundings. Some china patterns are timeless. Think of tiny, exquisitely painted flower sprigs on delicate porcelain cups. Who would not want to sip tea from one even while reclining on an uncompromisingly chic and modern sofa! The point is that anything which is functional is best used and enjoyed, not displayed in a glass-fronted cupboard. You can find new ways to show off family heirlooms. An oversized serving platter with a beautifully drawn floral pattern or banded motif could be hung from the wall or used as a fruit bowl, for example.

Adapt the display to suit the style of the piece. Contemporary vases are best left plain and empty so that they take on the guise of a piece of domestic sculpture. If they are used for flowers at all, a single stem or two of a striking architectural plant, such as cow parsley or fennel, is the only decoration that is needed.

These tall and elegant
vases make a dramatic
statement even though
they are quite simple.
The arrangement proves
that pairs of objects
have far more impact
than one on its own.
Images of flower
seed-heads have been
fired into the subtle
matte glaze. Flowers
would only serve to
interrupt their
uncluttered lines.

cool and clear

Strong marine and denim blues make an uncompromising presence

in any interior. Used well, they are positive and practical. To keep

the feeling fresh, soften deeper blues with the warmer hues of pale

parma violet and gentle hyacinth and forget-me-not.

Deep blues are not common in nature except in certain flowers, such as delphiniums, hyacinths and cornflowers. Paler blues, such as forget-me-nots, bluebells and scillas, are more frequently found in the plant world, but all blue flowers, for some reason, are beloved by gardeners, possibly because there are fewer true blue flowers than those of other colors.

Our references to blue are more likely to be drawn from the sea or from the sky, although the rich subtlety that comes from washed and faded indigo has its roots in nature (indigo dye comes from a plant). Dark blues absorb an enormous amount of light – just watch how blue flowers disappear first from view in a garden at dusk while the pastel colors and white continue to glow as the light fades.

This tendency to absorb light means that large areas of dark blue can look heavy and forbidding in an interior if not tempered by paler shades. Different blues work beautifully together and there seem to be more variations in shades of blue than any other color. All the blues give a feeling of tranquillity to a room, soothing the senses and creating a feeling of space, like the infinity of a summer sky. So often chosen for bathrooms and bedrooms, blue deserves to be used more frequently in living spaces too, where, if it is freshened with lighter shades of lilac or by the addition of white, it has a contemporary and upbeat feel. Unusually, you can successfully mix a shade of blue that has lots of green in its make-up with one that has pink in it, or with a soft violet or heliotrope. Flowers can be a useful device for balancing amounts and depths of the various color choices.

Strong blue is an uncompromising color to deal with but when it works well it looks superb in any style of interior. Though the Georgians loved to use it on interior walls, large-scale use of deep blue has never been very popular. This probably stems from the assumption that blue is a cold color, best used in small amounts for detailing, and never in chilly north-facing rooms. If you love the color blue, use it generously but remember to keep a light touch with the other surfaces and accessories that surround it. Break up very large areas of dark blue with paler shades of white or cream, and maybe use blue primarily in fabric furnishings and accessories rather than for large areas of painted or papered wall surface. The darkest shades of blue are better used in large rooms that have plenty of natural daylight.

When using a dominant color, do not overdo it. A single handsome armchair, perhaps, could be loose-covered in a modern washed-denim floral design. If you pick a fabric that is pleasingly coarse-textured with slight irregularities in the weave, the color will not look so deep or dense.

If you use these deep blues, keep the background of the room clean and bright. Floor coverings in natural, simple materials – wood, sisal or stone – will help to create a sense of space and throw the furnishings into clear relief. Small touches can help to counterbalance the tendency of deep blue to dominate the room. A collection of old-fashioned blue and white china, simply arranged on a mantel, or a group of delicate flower prints in handsome wooden frames would serve as a useful counterpoint to the areas of strong color.

Isolated in this way,
an imposing armchair
makes the very most of
the fabric that is used
to cover it. In a room
with a lot of other
texture, color and
pattern, it would have
far less impact.

RIGHT

The smooth stone floors and warm, creamy white walls of this old farmhouse, coupled with the light streaming in through the French windows, provides just the right balance for the deep blue denim cover of this big comfortable Chesterfield sofa. It will soften and fade as it is washed and worn. The indigo tones are picked up by the sprays of 'Bees Blue' delphiniums in the window.

FAR LEFT

The contrast between
the blue and white
embroidered silk fabric
of the cushion, with
its simple white check
design and stylized
flower motif, and the
fake chinchilla throw,
pushes the texture of
each into sharp relief.

CENTRE

Similarity of form
creates a link between
the earthenware plate
and the wooden bowl.

LEFT

The smoothness of
the denim sofa cover
is emphasized by the
textural quality of a
knitted floral cushion.

45

Soft deep blues combine
particularly well with shades
of cream, as these hand-
painted traditional earthenware
plates demonstrate.

RIGHT

This early Georgian panelled room is the setting for a pair of Cubist armchairs. Their loose covers in sweetly pretty faded floral linen create a gentle accent in an otherwise stark interior. Two chunky oak stools make unconventional side tables while a cotton throw, embroidered with botanical-print-style flowers, softens the severe lines of the chairs.

The pictures pinned in a neat row along the mantel are made from pressed dried flowers mounted onto thick artist's paper that has been washed with linseed oil to give an antique appearance.

1 Play with the differences in scale, texture, period style and shade when mixing prints of the same color together in a room **2** The intricate construction and detail of a passion flower becomes obvious when it is used to decorate a simply wrapped gift box **3** Keep blue wall coverings lightweight and airy in pale shades of azure and sky blue **4** An antique bunch of violets, once used to dress a hat, looks lovely clipped to a plain parchment shade **5** Create a ruched cushion edging from a tube of fabric. Run a line of gathering stitches down the center of the tube and then stitch the ruched fabric to the seamed edge of the cushion

bright ideas

Flowers in shades of blue are quite rare in nature and all the more desirable for that. But flower designs in blue on fabrics and other materials are easy to find and consistently popular. Touches of blue are always pleasing.

3

4

5

RIGHT

A flash of bright blue brings an otherwise dark area to life. Flowers with vivid blue petals are just right for this purpose, like the delphiniums gathered together in handsome metal florist's buckets.

FAR RIGHT

The brilliant blue of borage is equally electrifying. Float the flowers in a glass of summer punch for maximum impact.

Strong blue is a good color for outdoor as well as indoor furnishings. Its clarity and freshness suits the outdoor life with its connotations of all things breezy, maritime and sporting. Blue canvas-covered garden chairs look bold and stylish among the predominantly green shades of a garden in summer, without providing too strong a contrast. Pattern in the garden should ideally be subdued and subtle, without too much contrast with any background color. We have all recoiled from the brash floral patterns in clashing colors that are so often used to upholster chaise-longues and garden chairs.

Garden furniture seen against a flowery setting obviously needs simpler fabrics than that which has green as the predominant background color. Although ordinary fabrics can be used outdoors, bear in mind that sunlight, even when quite weak, will rapidly fade many fabric dyes and will also rot the structure of the weave. Tough cotton, either plain colored or in traditional simple stripes, makes a practical and inexpensive choice. However, as long as you remember to bring fabrics in whenever it is wet and at night, then you can use any material you like. More delicate fabrics can always be lined with something cheaper and stronger to protect them and increase their useful lifespan.

A farmhouse hallway makes a good place to store old-fashioned flower buckets, and offers a suitably cool place to leave cut flowers to be conditioned before they are arranged. Florists' metal buckets, while essentially practical, are good looking enough for simple arrangements, the tall clean lines making an excellent foil for those statuesque summer flowers with magnificent spires, be they brilliant blue delphiniums, soft pink clary sage or velvety red gladioli.

The details and accessories that you include in a contemporary floral interior can be as lavish or simple as you like. Provided the background of the room is simple and neutral, you can afford to include detailing that is as rich in pattern and texture and as flowery as you choose. Accessories with a floral theme are not hard to find – they can be collected from every period and in styles that range from kitsch to country. China and glass are obvious examples where flowers are strongly represented as a theme, and more prints and paintings of flowers have been done than of almost any other subject. Floral china will have most impact in a room if the color palette matches that of the main furnishings. A lot of antique china tends to have multi-colored images with no single dominant color and although beautiful in its own right tends to look nondescript and lost when seen from a distance. Easier to display are pieces based around one or two colors. Look for the simple sponged or stenciled designs often found on country pottery and earthenware.

Embroiderers have long looked to flowers for inspiration. Small pieces of embroidery can be framed flat or mounted very simply as pictures to hang on a wall, or incorporated into the design and construction of a larger piece such as a cushion or throw. Complete garments that have exquisite embroidery on them, like a waistcoat, ethnic costume, or a gorgeous pair of gloves, can also be displayed in their entirety, either protected by a frame or just as they are, depending on the environment that they are being put into. Embroidered fashion pieces, such as antique bags and tiny evening purses, can still be found quite inexpensively and they can add a richness and complexity of detail to a plain and simple room.

LEFT

Enjoy the velvety texture
of fresh anemones.

BELOW

A tiny embroidered
evening bag makes an
attractive accessory
for a bedroom.

RIGHT

A generous plain cream upholstered bed has been dressed with antique sheets, dyed blue, and a bedspread made from an old chintz frilled curtain. For warmth and coziness a cream quilt, delicately embroidered with sprigs of flowers, covers the bed and pulls the color theme together.

RIGHT

A simple iron bedframe is enlivened by an exquisite Marinekko floral cotton fabric used as a bedspread. Contrasting textures and floral patterns in tones of the same hue add variety to an interior without it looking fussy or ornate.

A sweetly pretty floral cushion in a delicate shade of mauve, together with a stem of an artificial orchid twining around a light cord, are the only other feminine touches in this otherwise austere bedroom.

FAR LEFT

In shades of violet, soft mauve and blue, these delicately patterned and padded fabrics and throws would make the perfect complement to a deep blue bedroom.

CENTRE

The delicate mauve and pink flowers on a miniature porcelain cup echo the translucent colors of the sweet peas in a simple glass tumbler.

LEFT

A plain white lampshade has been decorated with computer-generated floral images in subtle pale mauves and sugary pinks.

A child's fresh and
spontaneous floral images
created in chalk on a large-
scale blackboard wall.

Flowers have inspired artworks of all kinds from intricate and botanically accurate drawings to painterly sweeps of abstract color, from formal arrangements by Dutch still-life masters to chocolate-box evocations of cottage gardens. Color has much to do with our motivation to record something as short-lived and as beautiful as a flower, although it is nearly impossible in paint or any other medium to capture the translucent quality of pigment in a flower's petals.

Children are instinctively drawn to painting flowers, inspired by their simple shapes and glowing colors. They will embellish a drawing of a house with a cheerful row of flowers standing alongside. Their works of art have a wonderful fresh appeal to them, and it is worth preserving the best of them and finding a suitable place to display them. In a family-friendly kitchen, why not use one wall as a huge blackboard area for scribbling and having fun, or make an equally large bulletin board for displaying children's works of art. Children need a serviceable area to paint and play, so a good quality pine table could be protected from splashes and spills by covering it with with a floral plastic cloth (sensibly secured in place by a row of drawing pins under the edge). Flowered oilcloth, often printed in bold patterns and bright colors, was a cheap and cheerful answer to keeping pieces of furniture clean before the days of man-made varnishes and protective surface treatments for wood. It was replaced regularly as it wore out and added a colorful high spot to what were often very drab and unexciting kitchens. Today, plastic-coated fabrics are as much used for the unpretentious and jolly effect they give to functional rooms such as kitchens and playrooms as for their usefulness in resisting spills and stains of modern family living.

bold and brilliant

Hot tropical colors clash and vibrate. This palette of searing

shocking pinks and vivid oranges combines the reds of roses

and poppies with touches of turquoise.

Percale
Pommiers

1938
130 cms wide

茉莉花茶
Jasmine Tea

The color references for this chapter might appear to break all the rules on color matching. They are the colors of the tropics, hot and saturated zinging shades that appear to vibrate alongside each other. There is nothing very natural or subtle about these colors yet together they have a vibrancy and energy that is infectious.

This look is about contrast: a turquoise-blue tropical sky framing the brilliant crimson of a spiky ginger flower or the golden-yellow flesh of a papaya against the bright green of a fresh banana leaf. This hectic color activity works because no one strong color predominates. The result is a finely tuned balance. Fabrics from the Far East artlessly combine their colors and designs in a bold but similarly appealing way. Our Western textile design heritage tends to greater subtlety and more muted hues, but we can understand a lot from studying just how other cultures choose and combine colors and the proportions in which they are used.

Other good reference points are the paintings of Gauguin and Dufy, along with artwork from the Caribbean, objects and designs from Mexico and South America and all things tropical. Search out old prints and pictures of colorful seed packets and illustrations of flowers from the 1930s and '40s and you will find a similar feel. In nature, look for clashing mixtures of zinnias, for example, or bright annuals such as nasturtiums, godetias and poppies. The colors red, pink and orange are the key to the look in this chapter, used either on their own or in bold combinations. Green plays a minor role, as does turquoise and yellow, appearing like the flash of a feather on a parrot's wing through a jungle of leaves and blooms.

RIGHT

The severe lines of this industrial-style radiator are knocked back by the vivid red rectangle of a dining chair placed centrally beneath a painting that combines the same hot and clashing colors. The rose motif on the plastic chair is totally unexpected on such a functional object but echoes the subject matter of the painting above, linking the two.

The hot and very up-front colors used throughout this chapter may not be for the faint-hearted yet they can often be easier to work with than more subtle and hard-to-define shades. At least you know exactly where you are with shocking pinks and brazen reds and your instinct will probably tell you when you have included enough of them. A good way to accommodate these colors is to use them on things that are portable so that if you suddenly find their intensity too great, you can move them around or even remove some of them, diluting the strength of color.

In the dining room on the previous page the tall wall panel painted bright pink is not fixed, but just leans against the wall, so that it can be shifted like a stage set in or out of the scene. It can be repainted when you are tired of it or even wall-papered in something totally different when your mood changes. This movable panel is also a great way of introducing daring new paint colors to a room.

Reds, oranges and pinks have a powerful effect on the mood of a room and, if color psychologists are to be believed, on the mood of the people in it as well. The classic example is the use of red as a dining-room paint color: it is supposed to stimulate an appetite and be conducive to sociability and conviviality.

Hot reds, pinks and oranges appear to bring the surface that they are on nearer to you, unlike cool greens and blues that seem to make surfaces recede and small spaces open out. However, if you really fancy painting a small room shocking pink or bright orange, then keep it simple and be sure to balance the strong color with plenty of white and neutrals.

RIGHT

Revamping a set of
kitchen chairs with a
coat of paint in clashing
colors directly inspired
by the casual mix
of flowers is simple,
quick and effective.
A Chinese dress fabric
covers the cushions
while the cerise-pink
painted panel leaning
against the wall
introduces a larger area
of strong color to the
white dining room.

LEFT

The intense scarlet, cerise and crimson of anemone and ranuculus petals prove how well these colors can work if you feel like a brave and bold color scheme.

1 French caféware bowls meant for café au lait or hot chocolate and decorated with a stylized red flower motif are used with translucent orange plastic-handled cutlery to spice up breakfast or any informal meal **2** Once you have confidence using these bold and tropical colors and designs, start to think about contrasting the textures of fabrics, too, such as combining this Chinese floral print with red dyed sheepskin **3** Nature has been providing us with colors bolder than most modern artificial dyes as these botanical specimen boxes demonstrate **4** A beaded flower attached to a concrete lamp base adds a feminine touch to a minimalist interior **5** Floral tree lights look good simply piled together in a silver bowl to create a novel table centerpiece

bright ideas

Glorious splashes of brilliant color energize a room. Even the smallest

touch of searing red or Schiaparelli pink will do the trick. Surround it with

plenty of white to prevent it from becoming overpowering.

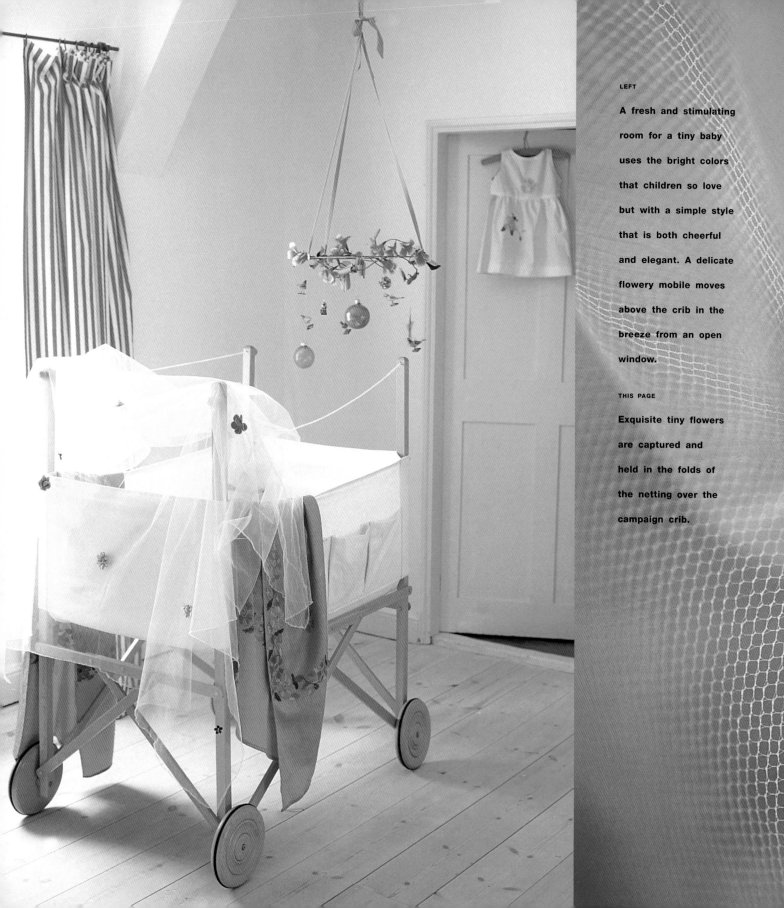

LEFT

A fresh and stimulating room for a tiny baby uses the bright colors that children so love but with a simple style that is both cheerful and elegant. A delicate flowery mobile moves above the crib in the breeze from an open window.

THIS PAGE

Exquisite tiny flowers are captured and held in the folds of the netting over the campaign crib.

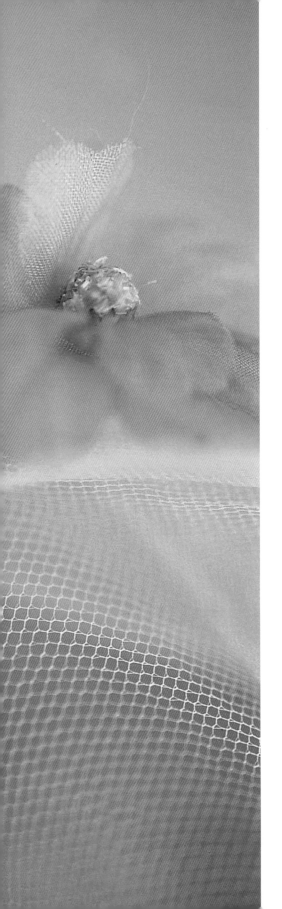

Children's and babies' rooms give you the opportunity to put together a scheme that does not have to be long term. As children grow they start to fill a room with the things they like and will possibly express an interest in how the room is decorated. While they are tiny, you can enjoy the freedom of making the choice for them.

In this child's bedroom the floral elements are kept very subtle. A strong color scheme has been chosen but it is a world away from the usual crude mix of primary colors – red, royal blue, bright yellow and green – that so often feature in children's rooms. It is always assumed that babies and children love strong colors exclusively but, just like introducing interesting new tastes and textures to their food repertoire rather than always giving into the bland, they are never too young to be surrounded with subtle and exciting color mixtures.

A nursery bedroom will have a fresh vibrancy if you base the color scheme on a wonderful mix of colors plus a large dose of white to keep the whole thing under control. Everything should be simple and easy to put together. Boldy striped curtains in cerise and white could be hung at the windows. Stripping the floor back to bare wood and painting the walls and woodwork pure white would give the room a sense of space and simplicity. You can then go to town on the baby's crib or bed by draping a delicate mosquito net over it. The whole net can be decorated with tiny multi-colored fabric flowers sewn randomly across it to add detail and interest while a mobile made from painted birds and Christmas baubles, hung over the baby's bed, would animate the room.

RIGHT

Orange velvet-clad bed bases are modernized and made practical with wheels in this twin-bedded guest room: a great idea where spare rooms are constantly being changed and re-organized. The bedding is a pretty summery mix of printed floral sheets found in Singapore, draped over the beds as covers, with cotton waffle blankets provided for extra warmth.

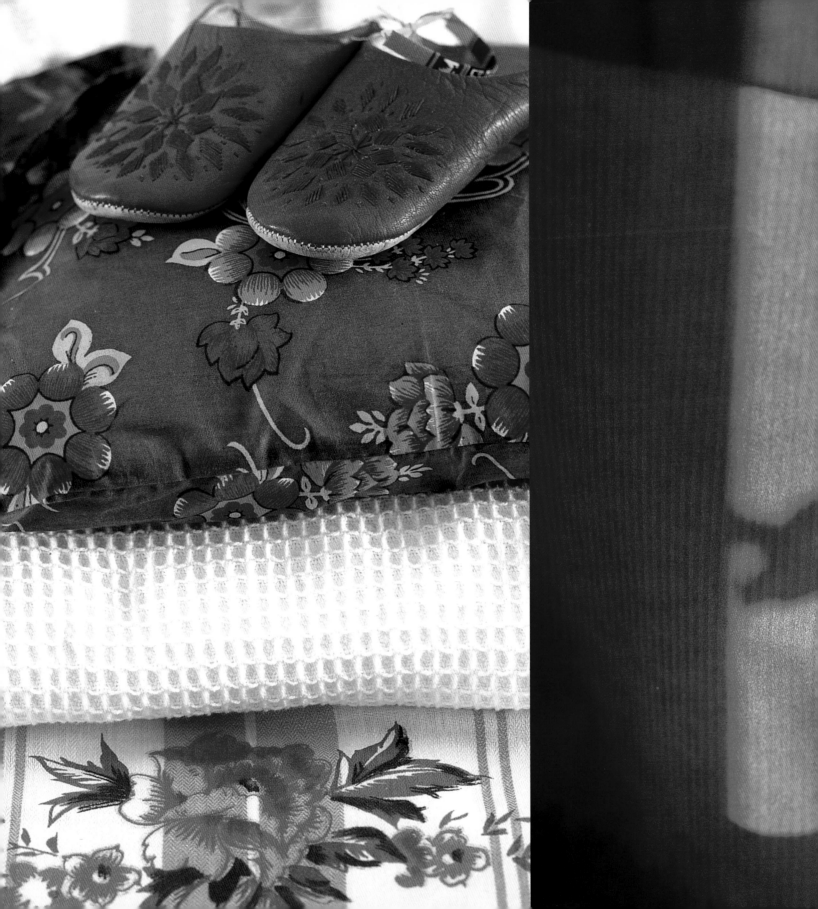

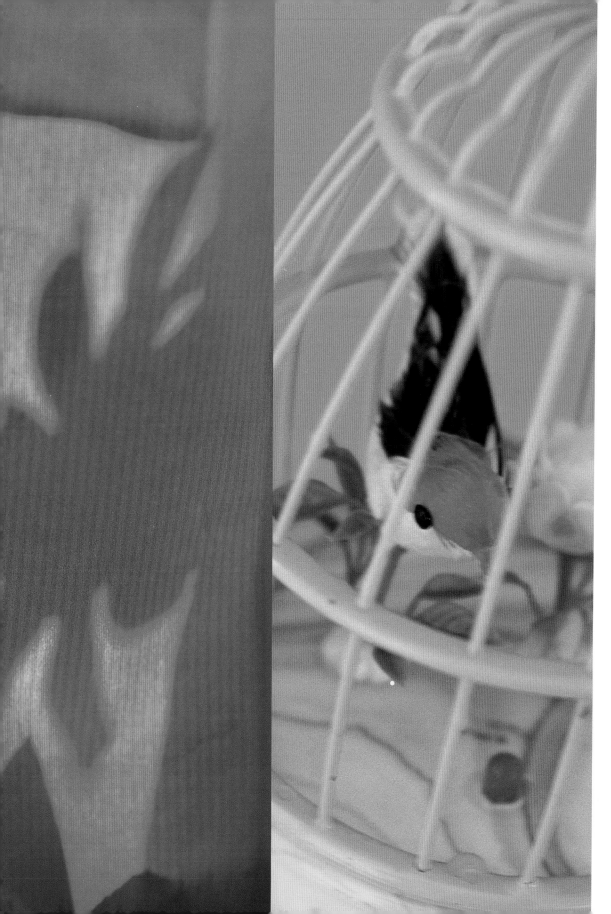

FAR LEFT

The bright and gaudy fabric prints from the Far East used for the guest beds on the previous page. Relief is introduced by fresh crisp white, waffle-textured cotton.

CENTRE

Red is the most life-affirming and positive color there is. Start by including a small amount of it.

LEFT

A slightly kitsch small singing bird in a plastic cage has an oriental feel to it.

RIGHT

The petal-shaped light
fitting brings a touch of
frivolity to an otherwise
Spartan room.

FAR RIGHT

Deep red walls painted
the color of old roses
provide a wonderful
backdrop for the clean
lines of a simple white-
painted table and
modern rubber vase,
with its ghostly stems
of flowers.

The balance of strong
color with white, coupled
with clean, straight lines,
gives this room a suitably
uncluttered feel. The
bright floral cushion adds
a note of informality.

A home office or workroom is one room in the house where brilliant color is never out of place. You are more likely to want to feel enlivened and motivated in a room designed for this purpose rather than soothed and comforted. A study or home office is a good place to experiment with color and pattern, even to fantasize a little. However, less is more and you do not want your office to look so busy that concentration is difficult, so keep the pattern to isolated areas.

To give an office a more relaxed feel, paint the walls a feminine pale rose-pink. The floorboards can be bleached for a lighter effect and the main pieces of furniture painted white for the same reason. Instead of an official-looking desk, use a simple and inexpensive folding table that is roomy and sturdy enough to provide plenty of work surface to spread out upon. A pretty country-style wooden kitchen chair in place of the usual office chair will make the room feel homey and not too efficiently functional. Cushions and a fabric-covered seat give the chair enough comfort for long sitting sessions as well as providing a place to use colorful fabrics. It is a good idea to mix functional stripes with interesting floral patterns, ensuring that the two are connected by their similar use of colors, for example, or their textural qualities.

Objects not normally associated with an office can be used for storage and to add warmth to the room. An old white-painted wirework jardinière would make an ideal home for inspirational bits and pieces and will also help to keep clutter in one easy-to-find place. Other equally attractive second-hand bargains can be used for storage. A Victorian flower-painted jug would make an attractive holder for pencils and pens.

Outsize flower prints fill a
whole mantel. Left plain and
unframed like this, they
become very much part of the
whole decorative scheme, not
just an added accessory.

RIGHT

Brilliant orange roses
vibrate with color
against their green
foliage. Flowers used
as simply as this and
tucked in against
everyday objects have
greater effect than
a fussy arrangement.

LEFT

A flamboyant Victorian
jug smothered with full-
blown pink roses makes
an unconventional home
for office supplies.

soft and subtle

Cool tawny browns and

the colors of earth and

stone. We are so used

to them that we may take

them for granted yet

these natural shades are

satisfying and gentle to

live with, especially when

punctuated with touches

of lively mauve and

warm yellow.

Recently, rich browns have reappeared in contemporary interiors after a spell out in the cold. This time around they have a subtlety and warmth not seen in their previous incarnation in the 1970s. It could be that the earth shades feel contemporary again because they are often part of a new textural story, bringing with it a complexity and depth that was lacking in minimal interiors. Think of smooth suedes and soft fake furs, slubby linens and plushy velvets – textures that add vibrancy to a color that would otherwise seem dead and lifeless on a plain and matte surface. In fact, earth browns do have life in them if they are highlighted with other natural shades, such as soft pollen yellow or a contrasting color such as parma violet or mauve.

Take time to look at the range and beauty of browns in nature, from the silvery gray-brown of ancient tree bark to the almost spicy brown of peat or newly ploughed winter fields. Few flowers are truly brown though there are a couple of old rose varieties that fade to a delicious shade of café au lait and some violas have a rich burnt orange color that is almost toffee-like. You can also find some varieties of iris in this same desirable and unusual color and big blowsy sunflowers appear in mahogany and ginger. Leaves are a different matter and by the time autumn and winter come they have taken on dozens of different shades from pale straw and burnt orange to deep rich chestnut and magenta.

Waxed and polished wood never goes out of fashion, bringing more brown tones into an interior. If your room includes these materials from the start then use them as the anchor and choose your other shades sparingly.

Most countries in the world which possess the raw ingredients to make ceramic wares have developed shapes and patterns that are distinctively their own. From the earliest days of making pottery, craftsmen discovered the possibility of using different-colored glazes to make their pieces distinctive and beautiful. Artists have always turned to nature for inspiration and potters are no exception. Flowers and foliage figure time and time again as motifs for the decoration of domestic pottery from humble plates, cups and bowls to grander vases and containers, as well as one-off designs. The decoration may be as simple as a mark made by a finger dipped in clay slip on a shallow bowl or as complicated as a portrait of an exquisite rose painted with a fine sable brush on a delicate porcelain dinner plate.

Domestic flatware these days has to be robust and practical. With few people prepared to go to the trouble of setting a full-scale table to eat at, most prefer to use simple pieces in plain glazes that can be put in a dishwasher and replaced easily if broken. But plain cream or white china, while being totally practical, is also dull. It is good to have a set of something more decorative, even if it is simply a mismatched collection of shapes and designs based around one color theme. The traditional country china originally hand painted in Maastricht in Holland has the bold good looks and painterly floral designs that fit easily into a modern interior. Examples of this style of pottery can be found all over the world. The basic design is much the same each time but the details and colors can vary slightly. It is easy to collect and looks good massed together stacked onto open shelves or single pieces can be mixed with plainer pieces to inject color and pattern into a neutral scheme.

The robust shapes of these simply painted earthenware bowls match the clean, sturdy lines of the simple wooden table.

RIGHT

In this cool and understated sitting room, the sofa has simply been draped in antique linen sheeting, with a length of natural-colored crewel-work fabric used to cover the seat. Crewel-work traditionally uses flower and leaf shapes to create the beautifully textured raised design. Soft ticking cushions and a natural sheepskin coordinate the look.

LEFT

Propped against the
wall behind the table
is a large-scale floral
picture, made by
projecting an image
onto canvas, which is
then painted. Although
both the fabric on the
sofa and the painting
are flower-based their
'florality' is subtle and
not overdone. A bunch
of flowers would not
have been nearly as
effective in this setting
as the branch of oak
leaves with their
strong, recognizable
outline.

95

The sweep of long curtains has a restful and soothing effect on the eye. It is a classic look that can still be very contemporary depending on the type of fabric chosen.

Well-proportioned windows with a good view, provided they are not overlooked by other houses, rarely need a curtain or blind, especially during the lighter summer months. Those living in colder climates like the security and feeling of comfort that curtains give a room during the long winter evenings when large areas of naked window panes are chilly and uneasy on the eye. In many houses what is needed is the option to blot out a less-than-perfect view in a casual and informal way. This could be achieved with a blind plus curtains or an arrangement of layered curtains that can be drawn or pulled back, depending on the situation. Blinds have a crispness and formality that does not suit every kind of window and style of room but curtains are more adaptable and can project any look you like depending on the how they are constructed and the type of fabric chosen.

In a house belonging to a friend, a high-ceilinged dining room that sometimes doubles up as a workroom has been given a dramatic treatment. The floor has been painted in a powerful and classic large-scale black-and-white diamond check. Equally bold and simple elements are needed to balance such a strong look. Floor-length outer curtains made in silk and jute are hung from a pole fixed well above and beyond the window frame so as not to take too much light. Inside these is a second pair set into the frame. The outer curtains have a large-scale design and the inner ones are made from a smaller coordinating print from the same design collection. The inner set can be drawn whenever more privacy is needed. The rest of the room is treated very simply with the walls painted off-white and a large functional but handsome table in warm cream making the centrepiece.

This whole room is a subtle mix of visual and textural contrasts from the ponyskin-covered chair to the smooth wooden vessel with its spiny artichoke within. Cozy but practical check tweed slippers are given a surprising twist with two luscious silk flowers. The black and cream flowery chenille rug makes a counterpoint to the polished oak floor beneath it. Delicate silk organdie makes an unexpected cushion cover for the ponyskin chair.

A mixed collection of different types of flowers in one arrangement will have less impact than a single very special bloom. Part of the philosophy of this book is to give interiors a more contemporary feel by allowing objects to breathe in plenty of their own space. Lightness and whiteness around a stem or branch will throw the flower into relief, isolating and highlighting its shape, texture and color. In this way, flowers can add a sense of drama and form to a room rather than being seen as just a pretty but shapeless mass of color.

To make a statement in a dining room with a long narrow table, you could use a fabric runner in a rich shade of purple and a fine glass vase holding just one magnificent long-stemmed hydrangea in shades of green, bronze and pink. The flowers chosen can pick up the colors of the china when the table is set for dinner.

Flowers destined for this treatment obviously need to be sufficiently long stemmed and stiff to stand upright. There are lots of other flowers that would suit this treatment although few are as texturally complex and as colorfully interesting as the mop-headed hydrangea. Picked in early autumn hydrangeas will slowly dry out to a papery version of the fresh flower. Alternatively, in late spring, you could try any of the really large-headed alliums in purples or greenish-whites or, in late summer, blue or silvery white agapanthus. In high summer, artichoke or cardoon flowers with their stiff stems and armadillo-like buds are lovely and last for days and days, gradually opening at the center to reveal the brilliant purple petals inside. Sunflowers are another generously sized flower with enough charisma to stand up to the single-stem treatment.

Forget the old rules
of having only low
flowers arranged on
a dining table. Use one
single flower instead,
for maximum impact.

LEFT

Lusterware china has a
richness and subtlety to
it that deserves close
examination.

Sun streams into
this airy bedroom that
feels filled with light
and space.

In a perfect world,
where there are
flowers, there will be
butterflies, but there
are more butterflies
on this lovely summer
frock than there are
real ones on the wing
most summers now.
A vintage clothes shop
find, this dress was
simply too beautiful to
resist buying and too
beautiful to be shut
away in a wardrobe.

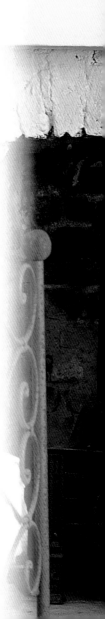

There is a danger with florals that, if they became the major part of the scheme, the completed look can just be too sweet, too pretty and too feminine. Patterns of any kind are demanding on the eye and generally we do not want our surroundings to be so visually demanding that they take over. Be aware of this and keep strict control of the amount of flowers and floral images you include and the way in which you use them. The colorings you choose should be part of this restraint which is why this book sets out to guide you into choosing the right color combinations. The flowers should never become the first thing to strike you on entering a room, rather they should be the elements that bring color and visual interest to the space in a subtle, but nonetheless unmistakable way

Bedrooms are probably the rooms where the most floral fabrics and wall coverings will be used. To counterbalance too much sweetness, keep other elements simple. The move away from fussy floor coverings towards stripped bare boards and hard surfaces means that you can indulge your taste for flowery fabrics without the risk of material overkill. If the thought of cold toes on bare floors in the mornings is less than appealing, then provide a neutral chenille or sheepskin rug at the side of the bed. Having fresh flowers in a bedroom is a worthwhile small luxury. Once you are in the habit of putting a single bloom or a little posy of something sweet and scented beside a bed or on the mantel you will realize it takes hardly any time and is always worth the effort. Find something from the garden or take one bloom from a larger spray of flowers destined for elsewhere in the house, or buy a single but exquisitely beautiful bloom from the flower shop.

1 A slip-decorated shallow bowl makes the perfect place for soap and hand towel in a guest bathroom **2** Scrunchy white linen covers an old armchair and, to provide a sensuous touch, a fur throw lined with a faded old-fashioned floral is piled onto the seat **3** Beautifully designed and printed fabrics need only be used in small quantities to bring the floral element into any room **4** The warm ginger brown of this crisp linen print cloth almost camouflages the rustic loaf with a crust in the the same warm shades **5** Reproduction hand-painted tiles of parrot tulips are so beautiful they are probably best left off the walls. Think of them as a work of art propped up on a mantel

bright ideas

Tawny browns, sepia and umber and all the shades of toffee and spice are wonderful colors to live with. Elemental yet easy on the eye, they make no great demands and small touches in the form of clever ideas and simple accessories add sophistication.

A bathroom dressed in
rustic browns and heavy
creams. There are
rough linen towels to
wake the senses,
satisfyingly rounded
woven lidded baskets
to store clutter and
a quirky knotted-string
chair. The old English
enamelware jug on
the windowsill offers
a permanent display of
seasonal flowers –
sunflowers in summer,
a spray of rust-colored
berries in autumn or
pale tulips in spring.

The range of colors and tones in all the different woods used in interiors is enormous. From palest ash to deep rosewood, well-kept, polished wood has a richness and subtlety like no other material. We often tend to take the natural beauty of wooden floors for granted, being so used to living with them and frequently failing to notice their effect on the other colors and textures in a room.

If they are in good condition and worth highlighting then make sure that they become a part of a coherent whole when it comes to decorating. To work with wooden surfaces already within a room, choose browns that have life in them, such as those with a hint of red that adds a spiciness, rather than those veering towards gray that can look very dead used in large amounts. Lift big areas of brown, whether floors, furniture or fabrics, with touches of yellow, subtle mauves and spicier orange and toffee shades. Brown can be rustic and earthy, even quite ethnic in feel, or it can be as sophisticated as you like. This will probably depend on the accessories that you use and the materials that the main pieces in the room are made from. To give brown a contemporary feel, think carefully about the textures that you use with it. Coarse slubbed linens, cool crunchy cottons and rough sisal or string all work well with the smooth polished grain of fine old wood floors, but for a very sophisticated but traditional look deep, dark, velvety petalled rich flowers can recreate the atmosphere of a Renaissance painting, the luster of the petals echoing the sheen of highly polished fine wood. Tall spikes of flowers such as foxgloves, delphiniums and foxtail lilies all have the height to make them something special but one alone, even in a very narrow vase, can look a bit thin. Better to use these giants in a group of three or more.

RIGHT

This hessian curtain, embroidered and printed with a naive floral design, sweeps in large loose folds to the floor.

CENTRE

Velvety soft beige suede covers a modern day-bed. The cushions are covered in a wool print in a curious color mix of yellows, greens and black that works beautifully with the stripped bare floors.

FAR RIGHT

The floral linen curtain is lined with a brown gingham that filters light through the weave.

deep and exotic

The bold contrast of black with white is a combination that makes

some of the most dramatic interiors. Bring the red of velvet-petaled

old-fashioned roses and the inky purple of the duskiest violas into

the picture to add spice to this palette.

PATTERN

FLOWERS

Souvenir

Painters used to be taught that pure black in a color palette was of little use to depict nature. Black flowers are never truly black but rather the deepest shades of inky purple or darkest burgundy. Throughout the centuries plant breeders have, nonetheless, tried to achieve the perfect black bloom knowing that the exotic and rare will always command an exceptionally high price. Black tulips are, in truth, a particularly dark shade of plum though certain violas are very nearly true black. Over the last decade gardeners have picked up on this dark and exotic theme once again, perhaps as an antidote to the popularity of silver, white or pastel herbaceous borders. As a result, certain flowers, such as the chocolate cosmos, black parrot tulips and inky dark regal pelargoniums, have been all the rage in the choicest borders and pots. But herbaceous borders filled with large amounts of 'black' flowers need the contrast of green or silver foliage to throw them into relief or a counterpoint of a strong red or burgundy to make some sense of the the whole idea. Just so in an interior where black and white are the main colors used. They need the spice of a little red or magenta to intensify the black and to add the necessary spark like the vibrancy of red lipstick on a dark-eyed, pale-complexioned face.

Black and white has always been a fresh and popular look whether it is the checkerboard floor of a 16th-century Dutch interior, the ebony and ivory style of a 1930s hotel or the sleek combination of white tiles and black metal or ponyskin fabric we might see today. Imagine any of these images, then add a vase of red poppies to the scene in your mind's eye. This one apparently minor detail lifts the look from the simply chic to the truly exciting.

Large high-ceilinged rooms give you the opportunity to use bold colors and modern floral fabrics. In my own house, a room converted from an old farm building into an office and day room offered the ideal opportunity to experiment with strong color. With light streaming from windows ranged all along one side of the room, a brilliant hot pink was used to paint a tall utilitarian cupboard and for the simple plywood stacking chair. The industrial style braces criss-crossing the ceiling make strong patterns in the roof space so equally definite lines and strong shapes were needed below them to counteract their visual dominance.

The wonderfully large sofa, big enough for several people to sprawl across it, creates a huge area of comfort and refuge at one end of the room. The fabric used for the cover is a very practical and hard-wearing modern linen and cotton weave with large scattered flowers in subtle gun-metal gray woven with a warm beige. Punctuating the solid gray of the sofa cover is one brilliantly flowered cushion. Made long and low to echo the sofa's proportions, its isolated splendor creates a focal point in the room. The fabric is a simple cotton print with a lively design of sturdy dahlias in a range of colors from a rich Chinese yellow, soft aubergine purple, vivid orange and a glowing pink. The drawing and printing of the design is traditional in style but looks fresh and new owing to the white background behind the flowers and the form of the cushion itself. Restricting the use of a vibrant fabric to just one special place in the room is a great way to use a small piece. You can show it off, whether it has been bought as a remnant, cut from something else second-hand, or is totally fabulous but only affordable on your budget in a very limited amount.

LEFT

Shocking pink is a bold
but life-affirming color.
Less intimidating than
full-on red, it still has
the ability to cheer
people up, to put them
in a good mood and
to bring a smile. Here
a big bunch of flowers
standing on the long
trestle work-table picks
up the color theme.

THIS PAGE

A sophisticated and very subtle treatment for a modern sofa. The charcoal floral-print cover is unexpected but works well over such a large area. The cushions are deliberately large scale and asymmetrical which gives a looser and more modern feel to the room.

RIGHT

The ghostly brittle stems of wild parsnip have textured reeded stems that are suddenly thrown into focus when they are painted in colors inspired by the floral cushion. Use a matte poster or emulsion paint that has a chalky finish for the most striking effect.

It is now easier than ever to find smaller pieces of furniture and accessories in a wide range of unexpected colors. New materials, methods of manufacture and color finishes mean that there are many more things to choose from than was once the case. The plastic stacking chair used at the trestle-table work-desk comes in a large range of bold and beautiful colors and, thanks to its simple shape, works very well when combined with more or less any other style or period of furniture.

Don't be afraid to mix wood with metal, metal with plastic or any other material with what might seem to be another incompatible one. Just as fashion has taught us over the last few years to think eclectically and to mix color, pattern and texture, there are lessons to be learned from this approach in interiors too. It does make it easier to create these mixes if the space that you are working in is simple, with no overbearing features of a distinct period or particular style. Even if there are, these can be knocked back and made less obvious by using a unifying and neutral wall surface and as simple a floor treatment as possible. Good simple materials and finishes are the aim; keep the paintwork neutral and immaculate, and the wooden boards and furniture well polished. Each piece of furniture should have a simple kind of integrity to ensure that it looks as good standing alone as it does when mixed with other things.

In your eclectic room include a few accessories that are just there for fun. A few touches – such as a floral glass paperweight – add humor and personality to such a big spacious room. Animals, too, provide a comforting presence in a workroom provided they will leave you undisturbed.

Your home office will encourage creative work if it has a few light-hearted and friendly touches.

RIGHT

The simplicity of such a
black and white scheme
as this relies on
extremely good detailing
in the room itself.
Interesting paneling on
the walls, a handsome
half-glazed door and the
strong checkerboard
floor create the right
framework for an
abstract ethnic fabric
used on the armchairs
and a contemporary
fabric made into a big
soft cushion.

LEFT

Nature needs no
instruction in the art
of matching color and
form as the exquisite
shape, texture and
color of this lily
demonstrates. Observe
nature closely and you
will learn almost all
you need to know
about style.

The composition of the sinuous
shape of an inquisitive cat
against the stark simplicity of
the checkerboard floor has the
intimacy and tight focus of a
Dutch interior painting.

1 Keep children's artwork for its spontaneity, enthusiasm and innate sense of good design. Their vision of floral themes is usually original and beautiful **2** Plain brown box files, used to store household paperwork, have been customized with a different photocopied fabric design glued to the ends that will be on show on the shelf where they are stored **3** A single flower sprig from an old-fashioned scented pelargonium variety sits in a tiny colored glass amongst a row of empty ones, simply demanding attention **4** Hand-paint your own ceramic designs. Choose a simple floral motif and maybe try just black on white for a really professional finish **5** Experiment by painting dried stems and seedheads in interesting colors, such as shocking pink or bright orange, to add color and vibrancy to rooms in winter when fresh flowers are in short supply.

bright ideas

The combination of black with white never fails to look stylish. Use small amounts of this powerful partnership for accessories and small details in a plain white or neutral room. Spark it up with lipstick red or sultry magenta.

4

5

Now and again you come across a piece of fabric that is so beautiful it deserves to be framed. One of my favorites is a bold and simple abstract floral designed by Celia Birtwell, a famous textile designer in the l960s. Such is its quality that it deserves to be isolated and seen flat. In this textile, the images are printed on an off-white slubby linen, very like artists' canvas, and the printing captures the splashy brush strokes of the design that have been executed in black and deep cream. It makes an ideal centrepiece for a black and white room. All kinds of printed fabrics would be suitable for this treatment though large-scale abstract subjects are probably the most effective. It is a great way to include a fabric that you really love but feel unsure about using for curtains or upholstery. This monochromatic fabric design slips easily into its surroundings in an effortlessly chic black and white room. Nothing small scale and delicate would hold its own with the bold tiled floor pattern and clean white paintwork. Beneath the fabric painting, a narrow white-painted side table holds various bits and pieces and another piece of art provides the only other color in the room apart from a bright throw.

To make your own fabric picture, provided the fabric is sufficiently strong, you can simply staple it tightly over a made-to-measure frame. With a less substantial fabric, the piece may need to be backed with lining or buckram, or an iron-on interlining. When stapling fabric onto a frame, start at the center of one side and staple it in place, staple the center of the opposite side, then the center of the two opposing sides, and move out to the corners, again working on opposite sides. The finished artwork can then be hung or just leaned against a wall.

LEFT

A fabric design like this is a work of art, so display it as you would a painting. It completely transforms this room from one that is plain and simple to one that is brave and exciting.

FAR LEFT

Velvety black tulips have an exquisitely sophisticated air, entirely in keeping with the spirit of this room.

LEFT

Fragile cherry blossom blooms on wintry looking branches. Its delicate perfection has inspired generations of Japanese flower painters.

RIGHT

Sweetly pink floral china contrasts with the heavy masculinity of a dark wood chest of drawers.

Some of the darkest, almost black, flower colors are to be found in the viola family. Look out for these rare but exquisite inky black varieties. Larger pansies come in dusky shades of purple and indigo too. Enjoy their velvet-textured petals in little vases or scatter them across dark and glossy chocolate cakes or puddings.

LEFT

The light from a fine sash window, kept clear and uncurtained, falls onto the silvered metallicized floral fabric used to make a cloth for a narrow side table. The cloth has a subtle lining of sumptuously soft deep purple velvet.

RIGHT

This huge and
glamorous image of
a single hydrangea
flowerhead, hung without
a frame for the greatest
impact, demands a very
plain setting to show
it off to best effect.

It has long been a decorating maxim for a new home owner to buy a work of art and then arrange the decor of the apartment around it. It certainly makes for an exciting way of introducing floral images in a contemporary style into an interior if you look for paintings, drawings, prints and other work of art on a floral theme. Flowers as a subject for art tend to be painted in a traditional and representational style more often than an abstract one. But why not forget the rows of fussy flower portraits of the Redouté school and opt instead for wonderfully exuberant pictures that contain the essence of flowers and plants. Notable examples of the latter would have to include the outsize blooms painted with great panache by Georgia O'Keeffe.

Buying art of this kind is quite a commitment and you need to follow your own emotional response to the paintings. Surprisingly, a painting may not cost you much more than a well-made pair of curtains in a good fabric. Keep your eye open for news about contemporary art fairs, markets and exhibitions and try to visit art school end-of-year diploma shows for possible bargains by as-yet unknown artists.

It is important to give a large modern painting the space it deserves. Most look best hung on pure white walls. One of my favorites has an image of a pale hydrangea head against a severe dark background. It is strong, simple and exciting and leaves no doubt that this is a floral image for the 21st century. Such strong images cannot be surrounded by clutter, so keep the floors simple and remove any unnecessary ornaments from the room, so that the eye is not distracted from the simple bold statement made by the single painting.

The importance of contrasting textures in interiors has become very relevant over the last few years and looks set to remain so. In my own farmhouse, one of the bedrooms is a good example of this virtue. The floor has been painted glossy white, which immediately modernizes the room and makes it feel more spacious, as light from the one main window falls inside and bounces around the surfaces. The walls are painted white, too, while a simple four-poster bed is painted in a warm cream. The windows have a double layer of curtains: the main curtains in plain linen fabric are of this same cream and hung from thin metal rails that are neat and unobtrusive, while the liner curtain in a delicate voile has a pale botanical print, which adds interest.

On the bed itself, I have chosen to create a dramatic contrast of textures. A shiny nylon quilt cover in a soft pearly gray provides the base cover and on top of this is another quilt that is far more elaborate, this one made from a very old cotton floral fabric. These two contrasting fabrics give the room personality and drama. The juxtaposition of sleek shiny fabric against matte, and plain against patterned, adds tension and energy to the scheme. I avoided the temptation to drape the bed-frame in fabric. Leaving the tall verticals of the four poster unadorned gives the room a greater feeling of spaciousness. A 'flower'-shaped lampshade hangs from the bed-frame for bedtime reading, adding a dash of femininity, while the simplest of pedestal tables, round and white on a slim base, stands in the corner to take books and general bedroom clutter. The design gives the room a timeless feel because of its simplicity and feeling of calm, but still comes across as an essentially modern solution to decorating a small spare bedroom.

Moving gently
in the breeze,
sheer curtains
create a calming
atmosphere.

A chandelier with crystal
flowers introduces
a floral element into
a room in the subtlest
manner. This pale
turquoise version,
probably dating from
the 1920s, makes
a glittering centerpiece
to an otherwise simple
dining room.

LEFT

A bright pink length of organza printed with rose stems has been thrown over an old rustic table making one bold hot-spot of color. Amazingly comfortable white molded plastic chairs and white lilies provide the luxurious touches in this otherwise sparsely furnished and accessorized interior.

The ravishing color, wonderful scent and exquisite form of these roses embody everything that is deep and exotic in the world of flowers.

Anthropologie
Stores nationwide and catalog.
800-309-2500
http://www.anthropologie.com
Tabletop, home accessories, linens.

Aria
San Francisco, CA
415-433-0219
Antique garden and architectural
ornament, lighting, and furniture.

**Australian Fabric Wholesalers
Pty. Ltd.**
Abbotsford, Australia
(03) 9417-4333
Floral tapestries, chintzes, and silks
from around the world.

Banana Republic Home
Stores throughout North America.
(888) 906-2800
http://www.bananarepublic.com
Tableware, linen, home accessories.

Botanica
San Diego, CA
619-294-3100
Stylish floral design, smart, chic
accessories.

Britex Fabrics
San Francisco, CA
415-392-2910
http://www.britexfabrics.com
Large selection of fabrics from
around the world.

Calvin Klein Home
Stores worldwide.
800-294-7978
Tableware, linens, home accessories.

Chelsea Garden Center
New York, NY
212-929-2477
Indoor and outdoor evergreens,
trees, containers.

Chintz & Co.
Victoria, BC
250-388-0996
Floral fabrics and accessories.

Cost Plus
Stores worldwide.
800-777-3032
http://www.costplus.com
Home furnishings and accessories
from around the world.

Crate & Barrel
Stores nationwide and catalog.
800-967-6696
http://www.crateandbarrel.com
Home furnishings and accessories.

Designer Fabric Outlet
Toronto, Ontario
416-531-2810
Wide selection of designer fabrics.

Garden Home
Berkeley, CA
510-599-7050
Interior furniture, topiary,
orchids, accessories inspired
by the garden.

The Garden Trellis
New Orleans, LA
504-861-1953
Garden ornaments, old and new,
plants and flowers.

The Gardener
Berkeley, CA
510-548-4545
Fine merchandise inspired by the
garden, from rugs to vases, all of
impeccable design.

Ikea
800-959-3349
http://www.ikea.com
Contemporary home furnishings
and accessories.

Laura Ashley
Stores worldwide and catalog.
800-367-2000
http://www.laura-ashley.com
Stylish floral home furnishings
and textiles.

Pier One Imports
Stores nationwide.
800-245-4595
http://www.pierone.com
Colorful imported vases, cushions,
home furnishings, planters, etc.

Pottery Barn
Stores nationwide and catalog.
800-922-5507
http://www.potterybarn.com
Attractive, affordable furniture and
accessories.

Restoration Hardware
Stores nationwide and catalog.
800-762-1005
http://www.restorationhardware.com
Home accessories and furniture.

Smith & Hawken
Stores nationwide and catalog.
800-776-3336
http://www.smithandhawken.com
Garden accessories, furniture,
books, etc.

Target
Stores nationwide.
888-304-4000
http://www.target.com
Affordable, decorative home
furnishings and garden supplies.

Z Gallerie
Stores throughout Northern
California.
510-843-6685
www.zgallerie.com
Eclectic furnishings, art, home
textiles, and decorative accessories.

Cover Cushions fabric (archive) from Sanderson; **16** Tie-dye throw from The Cross; **18** Sofa by Terence Woodgate from SCP.; cushion fabric from Sanderson archive; Lim coffee table and Driade glass ware from Viaduct; cushion fabric (archive) from Sanderson; still-life painting by Sue Williams; **20** Carved wood stools and granito bowl from Pol's Potten; **25** Stainless steel bed and olive ash Brentwood stool from Parma Lilac; oak blocks from Twelve Mailorder; mohair throw from Sanderson; acacia duvet cover by Descamps; felt wool blanket from Mint; **26** Ceramic vase from Space; **27** Floral tea glass from Holland; **29** Printed wool throw from Mint; cardigan from The Cross; **30** Aluminium table by Maarten Van Severen, Cameleon chairs by Philippe Starck and glass bowl and plates, all from Viaduct; painting from The Cross; Vidar fabric at window by Sandberg; **31** Green vase from Mint; **35** Ceramic vases by Rachel Urbiniki; **41** Meisho fabric by Monkwell; faux-fur fabric from Alton-Brooke; **46/47** Photograph of dog by Nigel Shafran; **48** Salvatore chairs from Habitat; faded flora fabric by Bennison; oak stools by e15 from Viaduct; ceramics by Anne Musso; dried flowers mounted by Rosie Brown; **49** Fabrics (from left): Marguerite by Dominique Picquier from Jagtar; Aubrey voile by Liberty; Trevellas by Osborne and Little; bottom: faded floral by Bennison. Wallpaper: top, Hawthorn by Neisha Crosland; bottom:Romilly by Sanderson; velvet violets from VV Rouleaux; Uchiwa fabric by Designers Guild; **56-57** Bed from Habitat; table from Josephine Ryan; stool from Gurr & Sprake; bedspread by Chelsea Textiles; Spinnaker linen curtains from Osborne and Little; **58** Emerson ticking from Designers Guild; **60** Top: brushed cotton sheets from Empire catalogue; **61** Lampshade paper designs by Gunna Ydri; **68** Rose chair from Ever Trading; still-life painting by Sue Williams; **70** Oak table from The Conran Shop; **72-73** Red sheepskin from Jackson's; fabric from Minh Mang; boxed fabric flowers by Mina & Mone; Anne Chedeville light from Mint; beaded flower by Mina & Mone; flower fairylights by Sally & Lucy Madge from @work gallery; **76-77** Waffle blankets from The White Company; slippers from The Cross; **80** Petal light from Mint; **81** Rubber vase from Mint; **84-85** Poster photographs from Catherine Graitwicke; **92** Antique china; oak table and bentwood chair from Pol's Potten; **94-95** Light by Philippe Starck for Flos; crewel-embroidered fabric from Capsicum; **96** Table from Woodline International; curtains (outer) Cheetah and (inner) Killa fabric by Malabar Cotton Company; **98** Carpet from Outras Coisas; slippers from Mina & Mone; **99** Table and ponyskin chair from World of Wonders; fabric by Capiscum; wooden vessel from Pol's Potten; **102** Nakshe fabric by Designers Guild; **104-105** Olive soap from Mint; throw from World of Wonders; Bentwood stool from Parma Lilac; Fleur d'hiver fabric by Donghia; **106** Chair by Michael Wanders from Viaduct; **107** Curtain fabric: Napoli Hessian by The Natural Fabric Company; table from Woodline International; **108** Daybed from Habitat; Medallion cushions by Neisha Crosland; ceramics by Anne Musso; **116-117** Sofa: anenome stem fabric from Sanderson; cushion: Antibes fabric by Brunschwig and Fils; paper and raffia-edged cushion by Rosie Brown; **118** Glass paperweight from Caithness Glass; **120** Greensleeves fabric by Celia Birtwell; **122** Greensleeves fabric by Celia Birtwell; **127** Table by Anne Demeultser from Binneheis; Olympia fabric by Celia Birtwell; **129** Chest of drawers from World of Wonders; **131** Verdi chairs from Habitat; silver-embroidered organza from Liberty; **132** Verdi chair from Habitat; velvet throw by Neisha Crosland; Hydrangea (1997), oil on canvas, by Jo Self at Flowers East; toy chairs by Philippe Starck from Viaduct; **134-5** Bedcover from Habitat; petal lampshade from Mint; herbal sheer curtains by Sanderson; **136-7** Toy chairs by Philippe Starck from Viaduct; chandelier from Decorative Living; printed organza tablecloth by Rosie Brown; ceramics by Anne Musso.